To My Loving Woman + Friend

Please know that you "ARE" loved.

Please understand that life is a gift.

Please know that you are in all

OUR HEARTS.

And know that "God" goes with you

ALWAYS

love

P.R.G.

2002 April.

© 2001 by Barbour Publishing, Inc.

ISBN 1-58660-289-6

Cover art © Images.com.

All Scripture quotations, unless otherwise indicated, are taken from the HOLY BIBLE, NEW INTERNATIONAL VERSION®. NIV®. Copyright © 1973, 1978, 1984 by International Bible Society. Used by permission of Zondervan Publishing House. All rights reserved.

Scripture quotations marked KJV are taken from the King James Version of the Bible.

Scripture quotations marked NLT are taken from the Holy Bible, New Living Translation, copyright ©1996. Used by permission of Tyndale House Publishers, Inc. Wheaton, Illinois 60189, U.S.A. All rights reserved.

Scripture quotations marked NRSV are taken from the New Revised Standard Version Bible, copyright 1989, Division of Christian Education of the National Council of the Churches of Christ in the United States of America. Used by permission. All rights reserved.

Selections by Viola Ruelke Gommer are used with the author's permission.

Published by Humble Creek, P.O. Box 719, Uhrichsville, Ohio 44683

ecpa Member of the
Evangelical Christian
Publishers Association

Printed in China.

Thinking of You

Ellyn Sanna

HUMBLECREEK
INSPIRATION FOR LIFE

Out of the abundance
of the heart
the mouth speaketh.

MATTHEW 12:34 KJV

Thinking of You

Whenever I think of you

   . . .I remember the laughter we've shared.

   . . .I recall the burdens you've lightened.

   . . .I rejoice at the way our relationship continues to grow.

   . . .And I thank God for the way you've shown me His love.

I thank my God every time
I remember you.

PHILIPPIANS 1:3

Thinking of You

How vast a memory
has Love!

ALEXANDER POPE

God gave us memories
that we might
have roses
in December.

JAMES M. BARRIE

<u>Shared Laughter</u>

Our mouths
were filled
with laughter,
our tongues
with songs of joy.

PSALM 126:2

When I think of you, I always smile.
I remember the silly adventures we've had
together. . .the embarrassing moments that
sent us into giggles. . .the magic moments
when all we could do was laugh out loud
. . .the long talks that were always
sprinkled with laughter. You and I
have had so many reasons to laugh together.
The funny things just seem funnier
when we're together—and you help me
find the laughter that's hidden
even in my darkest days.
I am grateful for all the laughter
we've shared.

To have joy one must share it—happiness was born a twin.

LORD BYRON

Thinking of You

One can never speak
enough of the virtues,
. . .the power of
shared laughter.

Francoise Saga

Among those whom I like,
I can find no common denominator,
But among those whom I love, I can:
All of them make me laugh.

W. H. Auden

"[God] will yet fill your mouth with laughter
and your lips with shouts of joy."

JOB 8:21

"Blessed are you
who weep now,
for you will laugh."

LUKE 6:21

Therefore my heart is glad and my tongue rejoices. . . .
You will fill me with joy in your presence.

PSALM 16:9, 11

Thinking of You

Some days I can't see anything funny
about my life.
Talking with you, though,
I begin to see from a new perspective.
I stop taking myself so seriously—
and before I know it,
I begin to laugh.
After sharing time with you,
I return to my life
with a fresh outlook.
The world's not ending after all—
and God's love and joy
still surround me.
Thank you for sharing
your laughter with me.

One can bear grief,
but it takes two to be glad.

ELBERT HUBBARD

May you always fly
on wings
of laughter!

Angels fly because they take themselves lightly.

AUTHOR UNKNOWN

Lightened Burdens

Carry each other's burdens,
and in this way you will fulfill the law of Christ.

GALATIANS 6:2

You have been a creative force in my life.
Where I have experienced pain,
 you helped me find healing.
Where I have felt weakness,
 you have showed me strength.
Where I have experienced loss,
 you have helped me
  find renewed faith.
Your creative approach to life
 has changed mine for today,
  for always.

VIOLA RUELKE GOMMER

. . .My friends have made the story of my life.
In a thousand ways they have turned my limitations
into beautiful privileges and enabled me to walk
serene and happy in the shadow cast by my deprivation.

HELEN KELLER

Two people can accomplish
more than twice as much as one;
they get a better return for their labor.
If one person falls, the other
can reach out and help.
But people who are alone
when they fall are in real trouble.
And on a cold night,
two under the same blanket
can gain warmth from each other.
But how can one be warm alone?
A person standing alone
can be attacked and defeated,
but two can stand back-to-back
and conquer.

ECCLESIASTES 4:9–12 NLT

Thinking of You

Therefore encourage one another and build each other up,
just as in fact you are doing.

1 THESSALONIANS 5:11

" Trouble shared
is trouble halved . "

DOROTHY SAYERS

Holy friendship that has medicine
for all the wretchedness is not to be despised.
From God it truly is, that amid the wretchedness of exile,
we be comforted with the counsel of friends until we come to Him.

RICHARD ROLLE

At times my life seems bitter to the taste.
At times my cup of life seems empty.
We share who we are in conversation,
As we speak of life, its gains and losses.
And my cup is refilled.
The taste of bitterness turns sweet.
You are good medicine.

VIOLA RUELKE GOMMER

A cheerful heart
is good medicine.

PROVERBS 17:22

There are "friends" who destroy each other,
but a real friend sticks closer than a brother.

PROVERBS 18:24 NLT

Trouble is the sieve
through which we sift
our acquaintances.
Those too big to pass through
are our friends.

ARLENE FRANCIS

Thank you for always sticking with me!
Please know you can always count on me
to be there when you need me.

Thinking of You

Growing Closer

"Let us journey on our way,
and I will go alongside you."

GENESIS 33:12 NRSV

As the years go by, I find I appreciate you more and more.
Our relationship has changed and grown,
as each of us has changed and grown,
as well. I'm glad we haven't outgrown each other.

Thank you for accepting the ways I've changed over the years.
I rely on your understanding of who I truly am inside my heart,
despite the external changes.
In a world that whirls so quickly 'round me,
I count on you as one of the stable constants in my life,
someone I can always count on no matter what.

As time brings new experiences to us both,
please know my love for you will never change.
I'm looking forward to growing even closer.

Thinking of You

Time shared with you is precious.

No need to explain.
You seem to hear my thoughts.
No words need be spoken.

Time shared with you is precious.

Peace and joy
fill my heart
once more.

VIOLA RUELKE GOMMER

If you have any encouragement from being united with Christ,
if any comfort from his love, if any fellowship with the Spirit,
if any tenderness and compassion, then make my joy complete
by being like-minded, having the same love,
being one in spirit and purpose.

Each of you should look not only to your own interests,
but also to the interests of others.
Your attitude should be the same as that of Christ Jesus.

PHILIPPIANS 2:1–2, 4–5

Thinking of You

One day held the memory of you. . .
And sowed the sky with tiny clouds of love.

ROBERT BROOKE

Hand grasps hand,
eye lights eye. . .
And great hearts expand,
And grow. . . .

ROBERT BROWNING

But, after all, the very best thing in talk, and the thing that helps the most, is friendship. How it dissolves the barriers that divide us and loosens all constraint and diffuses itself like some fine old cordial through all the veins of life—this feeling that we understand and trust each other and wish each other heartily well! Everything into which it really comes is good.

HENRY VAN DYKE

Do you know
that conversation
is one of the greatest pleasures
in life?

SOMERSET MAUGHAM

When I say, thank you for your smile,
You say, pass it on.
When I say, thank you for your listening ear,
You say, do the same for another.
When I say, thank you for your encouragement,
You say, offer the same to someone else.
When I say, thank you for keeping my secret,
You say, do the same for someone else.
Your simple example and quiet wisdom
Have taught me generosity of spirit.
Thank you. I will follow your lead.

VIOLA RUELKE GOMMER

One can never pay in gratitude:
one can only pay
"in kind"
somewhere else
in life.

ANNE MORROW LINDBERGH

"Do to others as you would have them do to you."

LUKE 6:31

Thinking of You

The heartfelt counsel of a friend is as sweet as perfume and incense.
As iron sharpens iron, a friend sharpens a friend.

PROVERBS 27:9, 17 NLT

Gratitude
is one of those things
that cannot be bought.

LORD HALIFAX

I cannot but remember such things were,
That were most precious to me.

WILLIAM SHAKESPEARE

I cannot imagine my life without you.
You are the one I call
when I'm delighted and proud—
and you're the one I want to talk with
when I'm crying.
I depend on you to understand
my thoughts and feelings;
I know on my hardest days
I can rely on your prayers
supporting me all the way.

I could get by with less money
and fewer possessions—
but I wouldn't want to get along
without you.
You are truly one of my life's
greatest treasures.

Our friendship through the years has made
Our patchwork lives into a lovely tapestry.
The threads woven through simple pieces of fabric
Are respect, affection, appreciation, admiration, support,
Comfort, forgiveness, patience, refuge, joy, and laughter.
These priceless threads of gold and silver
Strengthen and beautify the texture of our
Friendship. Each year the tapestry of
Relationship grows more valuable.

VIOLA RUELKE GOMMER

Keep on loving each other. . . .

HEBREWS 13:1

Never shall I forget the days
which I spent with you.

LUDWIG VAN BEETHOVEN

It is very easy to forgive others their mistakes;
it takes more grit and gumption
to forgive them for having witnessed our own.

JESSAMYN WEST

Thinking of You

"Stay"
is a charming word
in a friend's vocabulary.

LOUISA MAY ALCOTT

You have seen me at my worst—
and yet somehow, it never matters.
If anything, we just keep growing closer
the more painfully honest we are with each other.
Thank you for putting up with all my faults!

You are as welcome
as flowers
in May.

WILLIAM SHAKESPEARE

It suddenly seemed to me
that we had always been near each other
and that we would always be so. . . .
It was one of those tender and peaceful feelings
which are like a gift flowing from a region higher than ourselves,
illuminating the future and deepening the present.
From that moment our understanding was perfect. . . .

RAISSA MARTIAIN

How different we are!
You are tall, thin, fair,
and always on time.
I am shorter, wider, darker,
and usually late.
What makes us friends?
What makes us friends
are what we cherish—
Family, friends, and faith.
We may be different,
But we are soul close.

VIOLA RUELKE GOMMER

Words satisfy the soul as food satisfies the stomach;
the right words on a person's lips bring satisfaction.

PROVERBS 18:20 NLT

Only friends will tell you the truths
you need to hear to make. . .
your life bearable.

FRANCINE DU PLESSIX GRAY

Thank you for all the times you've said
exactly the right thing to me!
I pray our relationship will continue to grow.

I See God's Love Through You

No one has ever seen God;
but if we love one another,
God lives in us and his love
is made complete in us.

1 JOHN 4:12

I have learned that to have a good friend
is the purest of all God's gifts. . . .

FRANCES FARMER

"To see your face
is like seeing the face
of God."

GENESIS 33:10

Every true friend is a glimpse of God.

LUCY LARCOM

Thinking of You

Human love. . .
out of which are built the memories that endure,
are also to be treasured up as hints
of what shall be hereafter.

BEDE JARETT

"As the Father has loved me,
so have I loved you.
Now remain in my love.
My command is this:
Love each other as I have loved you."

JOHN 15:9, 12

How can I ever express how much you mean to me?
What can I do to repay you for all the hours of understanding?
You not only listened all those times when I was hurt or desperate,
excited or glad, but you cried with me, you helped me laugh again,
and you were more proud of me than I was of myself.
Can I put a price on what that meant to me?

Of course I can't.
What you have given me is not in the realm of dollars and cents,
or even the world of balanced trade.
Instead, our relationship belongs in the kingdom of God.
You give yourself with no thought of reward.

You show me God.

Thinking of You

I owe thee much:
thou hast deserv'd from me
Far, far beyond what I can ever pay.

ROBERT BLAIR

Many words
are meaningless.

ECCLESIASTES 5:7

Words are but empty thanks.

COLLY CIBBER

We always thank God for. . .you,
mentioning you
in our prayers.

1 THESSALONIANS 1:2

Whenever I think of you, I realize how much
I have learned from you.
You have shared your insights with me, your wisdom,
your understanding; you have taught me so much.
Most of all, you have helped me to see God's face.
So many times God used your hands to touch my life,
your words to speak comfort to my soul,
and your heart to bring me His love.

I guess that's why whenever I think of you, I thank God!

Thinking of You